100 Notes – 100 Thoughts / 100 Notizen – 100 Gedanken | №064

Brian Holmes

Profanity and the Financial Markets: A User's Guide to Closing the Casino / Das Profane und die Finanzmärkte. Eine Gebrauchsanleitung zur Schließung des Casinos

dOCUMENTA (13)

HATJE CANTZ

"Occupy Wall Street"
Zuccotti Park, New York
October 10, 2011 /
10. Oktober 2011

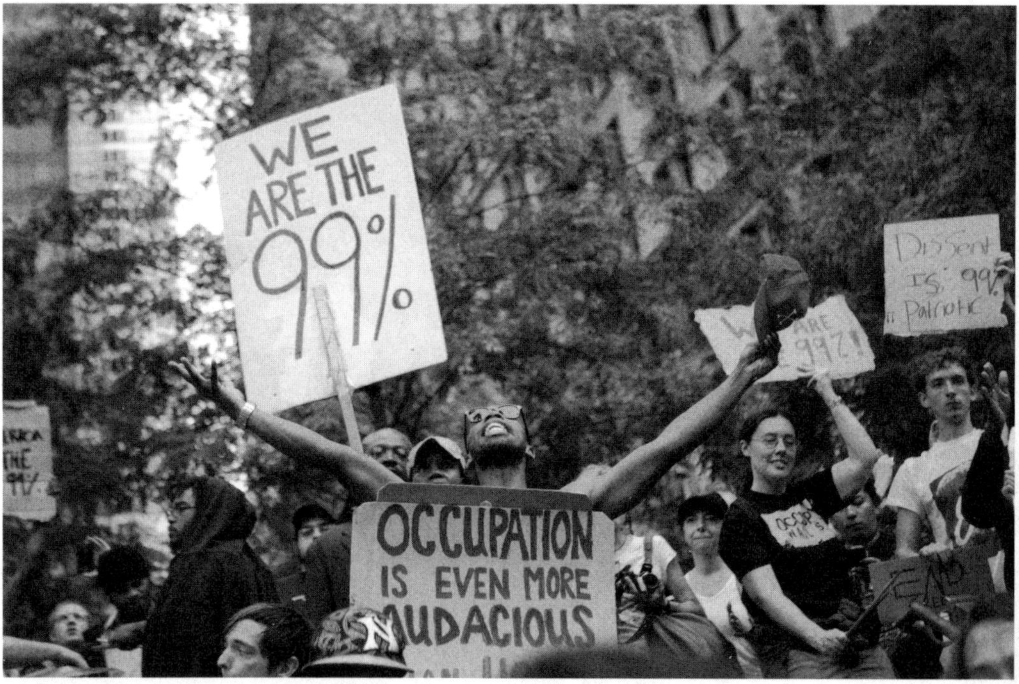

Brian Holmes

Profanity and the Financial Markets: A User's Guide to Closing the Casino / Das Profane und die Finanzmärkte. Eine Gebrauchsanleitung zur Schließung des Casinos

Brian Holmes

Profanity and the Financial Markets: A User's Guide to Closing the Casino

I want to begin, not with a curse, but with a very beautiful convergence—one widely held to be real, but shrouded in mystery for millions of people. I am talking about the "movement of the squares" unfolding on both sides of the North/South divide. What is the hidden link between the middle-class and precarious movements against the dictates of finance capital—Occupy Wall Street and the European Indignados—and the far more perilous struggles to end dictatorships in North Africa and the Middle East? What relationship could possibly be sustained between the regions that concentrate global wealth and those from which labor, resources, and interest payments are relentlessly extracted?

Immanuel Wallerstein claims that the uprisings in the Middle East and North Africa pit two historical groups against each other. One he calls the "1968 current," which consists of nonviolent, directly democratic grassroots movements that challenge all forms of exclusion and abuses of power, in the name of an equality that includes respect for fundamental differences. The other group consists of people who oppose such movements and seek in whatever way to capture, contain, and neutralize them—and in North Africa and the Middle East, that chiefly means holders of oil wealth and U.S.-backed dictators. For Wallerstein, today's uprisings are a continuation, after decades of latency, of "the world-revolution of 1968," which extended by his account from 1966 to 1970.[1]

If this is true, then the people out in the streets today at least share a history. Because the world-revolution of 1968 also took place in Europe and in the United States, where it revolved crucially around solidarity and direct cooperation between Northern middle-class students and intellectuals and oppressed people in the South—which in the U.S. meant not only Vietnam and Latin America but also the South of our own country. Whites went to Alabama, Georgia, and Mississippi to work with the civil rights movement. Oppressed minority groups, especially the Black Panthers, read Frantz Fanon and other anti-colonial thinkers and came to designate themselves as Third World peoples. The New Left sought to express its support for the Vietnamese revolutionaries by "bringing the war back home." A vast, unruly, and often failed experiment in cross-class, cross-border collaboration defined the "1968 current." But is this historical memory enough to explain the convergence of direct-democratic practices in the movement of the squares?

I do not think it is. To uncover the more complex grounds on which we meet, it's necessary to look back to the reactionary surge that followed 1968, ultimately giving rise to neoliberalism. It began in the U.S. with the election of Richard Nixon. He ran on a law-and-order platform, and his administration crushed domestic dissidents with covert operations, legislated "spatial deconcentration" programs for inner-city gentrification, invented SWAT teams for attacks on the ghettos, launched the prison-industrial complex, and offered support to the military regime of Pinochet in Chile, opening the door to the coordinated repression of the Latin American Left by Operation Condor in the later 1970s. Nixon also presided over the settlement of the 1973 Arab-Israeli war and the OPEC embargo. That led on the one hand to the U.S. stabilization of Egypt (with military aid formalized in 1979 as part of the Camp David accords) and on the other, to the new petroleum prices and the introduction of a capital circuit linking Western banks, engineering firms, and armament makers to the most oppressive oil-exporting regimes. The whole process cemented the position of authoritarian leaders in the Arab world and provided the cash for a major round of predatory lending to developing countries across the planet. The dictators who have recently fallen in North Africa and the Middle East date from this period. Thus both domestically and internationally, the 1970s saw the installation of a police and military order that sought, and still seeks, to capture and contain the "1968 current."

As police rapidly militarize in the North, the experience of repression becomes another thing that today's movements share—unequally,

1 | Immanuel Wallerstein, "The Contradictions of the Arab Spring," *Al Jazeera English*, www.aljazeera.com/indepth/opinion/2011/11/2011111101711539134.html.

as usual. Yet again, that's not the whole story, and a further moment of history must be considered. In the U.S. and throughout the developed countries, student protest and the emergence of a counterculture appeared to herald the rise of a "new class" capable of grasping the levers of power in increasingly bureaucratic systems. This new class consisted of administrators, scientists, engineers, educators, social workers, opinion makers, and artists.[2] It was nurtured in the liberal universities of the welfare state, at a time when the functions of government had dramatically expanded, leaving the old patricians behind. Decision making by committee had replaced the leadership of "great men," and the private ownership of corporations was increasingly considered a legal fiction.[3] To neoconservative eyes, the student revolt threatened to radicalize what was already a mainstream trend toward collective control of the American political economy. The societal struggle of the 1970s, at a time of deep economic crisis, revolved around furthering or blocking this possible takeover of power.

More recent sociological thinking observes that after the period of widespread alienation accompanying each major crisis, a reformed and transformed capitalist system has to succeed in reintegrating its qualified managerial and technical personnel along with the producers of artistic and intellectual culture.[4] The new order has to recover the confidence of those who will be charged with administering and reproducing its logic. How was this achieved from the 1980s to today, with respect to the professional-managerial classes of North America and Europe and, indeed, to similar strata in the developing world? The answer to this question will reveal both the glaring divide and the hidden links between the Northern and Southern movements.

Here's my idea: the integration of the professional-managerial classes into the neoliberal phase of capitalism has been accomplished by a complex but unified and deeply pervasive mechanism that may be called the financial apparatus. Or you could just call it the casino. Its operations can be felt across the spectrum of society, not only in business but in art, education, public administration, technology, the media, urbanism, diplomacy, and, most acutely of all, social psychology. The necessary converse of systematic military repression is an adrenaline-charged roll of the electric dice. When we occupy Wall Street in the global financial capital of New York City, or any other financial district in any other city, what we do is oppose the integrative strategy of those who seek to capture, contain, and neutralize the effects of world revolution. In this way we stand in solidarity with our brothers and sisters in North Africa and the Middle East (and in Latin America and other regions) by taking actions that are in no way identical, but instead run parallel to theirs. Could one cross the line to direct cooperation? Let us hold on to that question.

2 | Three books on the new class appeared in a single year: Pat Walker, ed., *Between Labor and Capital* (Boston: South End Press, 1979); A. W. Gouldner, *The Future of Intellectuals and the Rise of the New Class* (New York: Seabury, 1979); and B. Bruce-Briggs, ed., *The New Class?* (New Brunswick, N. J.: Transaction Books, 1979). The first reprints a crucial essay by Barbara and John Ehrenreich on "The Professional-Managerial Class," and the third gives neocon viewpoints.

3 | For the issues of ownership and control, see A. A. Berle and G. C. Means, *The Modern Corporation and Private Property* (New York: Harcourt, Brace and World, 1968 [orig. 1932]); James Burnham, *The Managerial Revolution* (New York: John Day, 1941); and J. K. Galbraith, *The New Industrial State* (Boston: Houghton Mifflin, 1967).

4 | See Luc Boltanski and Ève Chiapello, *The New Spirit of Capitalism* (London: Verso, 2005 [orig. 1999]), as well as my text "The Flexible Personality" (2002), http://eipcp.net/transversal/1106/holmes/en.

Global Gamble

Marxists like David Harvey interpret the financial turn that began in the early 1970s as a "class strategy" to restore the prerogatives of ownership, giving rise in our time to the power of the worldwide 1 percent.[5] Others such as Michael Hudson and the late Peter Gowan concentrate on the strategies of the American state: structural support for neoliberal finance is Washington's "global gamble" to maintain control over the international monetary system.[6] Gérard Duménil and Dominique Lévy integrate both approaches, but they also introduce a crucial class concept. In their view, Keynesian Fordism represented a compromise between the middle and working classes, while under neoliberalism (or what I call Neoliberal Informationalism) the middle classes have been sucked back into the service of capital.[7] In the art world, the multiplication of billionaire patrons and corporate museums makes that clear enough. But let's look at a more mainstream figure of this class compromise: the financial trader, who as the lowest rank of "golden boy" can strike it fabulously rich or lose big, burn out young, and fail abysmally.

With his eyes glued tightly to a personalized array of screens, the trader at a major bank or hedge fund is jacked into a transnational network comprising tens of thousands of institutions and millions of individual players. He works with stocks, bonds, and currencies, and increasingly with derivatives of these underlying values, created through the application of mathematical formulae. His activity locates him at the crossroads of two contradictory theories.

On the one hand, he faces streams of primary data that are considered entirely objective. They are prices, market facts generated by anonymous buyers and sellers whose collective judgment is supposed to provide real information about goods and services. Trading acts to smooth out minor differences in price through the process of "arbitrage": buying slightly lower in one place, selling slightly higher in another. In this way it is supposed to correct inaccuracies and perfect the system. The idea that market prices assure a perfect equilibrium between supply and demand, leaving only a residual fluctuation that is ultimately random, is known as the "efficient market hypothesis."[8] It underwrites an enduring faith in the neutrality of financial speculation.

At the same time, the trader is lionized as an exception, a maverick, a genius. He is possessed of unique knowledge, lightning speed, unparaleled aggressiveness, and an uncanny "feel" for trends. Through his manipulation of information that is theoretically available to everyone, the trader constantly creates value for the bank and its clients. He does so in

5 | David Harvey, *A Brief History of Neoliberalism* (Oxford: Oxford University Press, 2005).

6 | Michael Hudson, *Super Imperialism* (London: Pluto Press, 2003 [orig. 1972]); Peter Gowan, *The Global Gamble* (London: Verso, 1999).

7 | Gérard Duménil and Dominique Lévy, *The Crisis of Neoliberalism* (Cambridge, Mass.: Harvard University Press, 2011), esp. chs. 1 and 5.

8 | Justin Fox, *The Myth of the Rational Market* (New York: HarperCollins, 2009).

the strictest separation from the fate of any real goods or services, since he can make money on numbers going either up or down. He keeps his own book of profit and loss, and even though he is dealing with other people's money he must make singular and original choices, since he is rewarded for acting only on those particular risks where he can make a profit. The trader is defined by what economic theory deems impossible: the ability to "beat the house." Hypercompetition and virtuoso skill make him the middle-class hero of Neoliberal Informationalism.

How does a narrow class strategy, concentrated into specific persons and technical functions, spill over into an entire era and lend its coloration to a whole diffuse period of human coexistence? In a 1977 interview, Michel Foucault gave a definition of one of his key concepts: the apparatus. His discussion, though highly abstract, reads like a cartographer's key to our financialized society. The apparatus is the "system of relations" that knits together a set of seemingly unrelated elements: "a thoroughly heterogeneous ensemble consisting of discourses, institutions, architectural forms, regulatory decisions, laws, administrative measures, scientific statements, philosophical, moral and philanthropic propositions." It is a "formation which has as its major function at a given historical moment that of responding to an urgent need." Yet beyond this urgency, the apparatus is constructed to sustain both "a process of functional overdetermination" and "a perpetual process of strategic elaboration." Finally, Foucault notes that "in trying to identify an apparatus, I look for the elements which participate in a rationality, a given form of co-ordination [*une concertation donnée*]."[9] The aim is to grasp the operations of a ruling idea through an interlocking series of social forms.

After an initial study of the disciplinary device known as the Panopticon, Foucault turned his attention to the "security apparatuses" that are characteristic of liberal or laissez-faire economic policy. His first example was an eighteenth-century redevelopment plan for the city of Nantes, which involved cutting out new streets to serve four overlapping functions: the aeration of unhygienic neighborhoods, the facilitation of trade inside the city, direct connection to long-distance transportation networks, and the surveillance of traffic in an urban environment that is no longer walled or subject to curfew. Instead of developing closed, precisely defined spaces for exclusive uses, as in a disciplinary schema, the plan creates a series of multifunctional corridors that can expand in various directions, according to future patterns of growth that cannot entirely be foreseen. Government functions probabilistically, less as an instance of command than as an enabling framework for circulation.

The effect of the security apparatus is not to impose anything on anyone, but instead to select the most favorable elements from the

9 | Michel Foucault, "The Confession of the Flesh" [orig. 1977], in *Power/Knowledge: Selected Interviews and Other Writings*, ed. Colin Gordon (New York: Random House, 1980); translation slightly modified.

spontaneous behaviors of a given population and then shape an environment to optimize them still further, until their very predominance excludes unwanted traits. The idea is "to reduce the most unfavorable, deviant normalities in relation to the normal, general curve."[10] Outright repression continues to exist, but it is reserved for "dangerous" elements that could perturb the system. Over the past three decades, exactly such a schema has defined the preferred relations between the holders of concentrated capital and their servants, the professional-managerial classes.

10 | Michel Foucault, *Security, Territory, Population: Lectures at the Collège de France, 1977–78* (New York: Palgrave Macmillan, 2007 [orig. 2004]), p. 90.

Had Foucault lived through the speculative boom of the late 1980s, he would have recognized transnational finance as the crucial security apparatus of the neoliberal era. Computerized trading applies a logic of risk optimization to circulating capital flows, and it does so within precisely defined technological, informational, and legal environments. Let's consider how those environments emerged, after the collapse of the Bretton Woods fixed-exchange-rate treaty in 1971. The urgent need to which currency futures, options, and other derivatives responded was that of managing transnational business operations under conditions of unprecedented volatility, where values fluctuated hour by hour and prices were subject to multiple forms of risk. Sophisticated mathematical models combined with networked price-information systems not only helped to mitigate those risks by complex hedging strategies but also served to generate liquidity for a wave of mergers and acquisitions, at a time when corporations were scaling up to the global level. Yet the financial turn also fit into a larger strategy for the reintegration of the professional-managerial classes, whose younger elements had been alienated by the standardization and regimentation of Fordism.

The strategy hinged on the recognition of individual difference as constitutive of human capital, whose promised "returns" would be offered in compensation for the suppression of public facilities and entitlements. The fiscal crisis of the welfare state could be resolved if all the expenses of social reproduction—health, education, transportation, housing, unemployment, retirement—were assigned to individuals as investments in their human capital, for which credit could be furnished by private banks, at interest. Ideology, patriotism, and family values no longer had much sway over the members of the "new class," but the tantalizing prospect of accessing some speculative capital, combined with the monthly obligations of student-loan payments and homeowner or consumer debt, furnished more precise means of behavioral control. As the university retooled to serve the knowledge economy, the most popular artists and intellectuals became culture stars, and a few scientists began drawing major profits from intellectual property. And at the elite end of the social spectrum, ownership prerogatives were restored when shareholder value became the governing principle of enterprise. Instead of focusing on production, corporations would now pursue a single goal: generating cash, and therefore social power, for their owners.

These are tremendous changes with respect to Keynesian Fordism. But one could go further and show how the cybernetic calculus of finance operates as a coordinating rationality for just-in-time production, distribution, and sales. When the G-20 finance ministers strive to forestall a transnational credit crunch, it is this just-in-time system that they are serving. The rhythms of finance have come to govern the entire circulation system of the world economy.[11] However, if we want to understand how the social relations of the trading floor have spilled over to reshape contemporary culture—through a "functional overdetermination" of the financial apparatus—then we will have to turn back to the micro level and look more closely at what actually happens inside the casino.

11 | See my article "Do Containers Dream of Electric People? The Social Form of Just-in-Time Production," in *Open*, no. 21: "Im/mobility" (2011), www.skor.nl/_files/Files/OPEN21EN_P30-44.pdf.

12 | Karin Knorr Cetina and Urs Bruegger, "Traders' Engagement with Markets: A Postsocial Relationship," in *Theory, Culture & Society*, no. 19 (December 2002). All quotes in this and the following paragraph are from this article.

Starfuckers

The sharpest observations emerge from fieldwork by Karin Knorr Cetina and Urs Bruegger among a team of UBS currency traders in Zurich. What they claim to have discovered there is a "postsocial relationship": an intellectual, perceptual, and visceral interaction with the "market on screen," experienced by the traders as "a complex 'other' with which they are strongly, even obsessively, engaged."[12] According to these sociologists, the market that coalesces into presence on the screens is indistinguishable from a "life form," constantly fluctuating, elusively shifting and changing. Its complexity arises from a double aspect, for it is both a flow that one enters and alters and a quasi-conscious other that one encounters with a shock of recognition. As Bruegger and Knorr Cetina write: "the transfer of the market onto the screen has meant that traders are now able to simultaneously position themselves inside the market in the sense of becoming players in its overlapping networks, and to relate to the market on screen as an exteriorized other, a sort of master being that observes all transactions and includes their contextual conditions and motivations." The interaction with the market is tumultuous and passionate, oscillating between the desire and fear of volatility, the narcissistic elation of profit, and the violent shock of loss. Failure is expressed in graphic metaphors where sexualized aggression turns inward from the market to the trader: "I got shafted, I got bent over, I got blown up, I got raped, I got stuffed/the guy stuffed me, I got fucked, I got hammered, I got killed." All of that, remember, is happening at work, via an apparently cool and technocratic gaze on three or six or eight computer monitors.

Borrowing a page from psychoanalyst Jacques Lacan's text on the "mirror stage" of human development, the two authors compare this relationship with the market on-screen to the infant's relationship with its own reflection, experienced as the tantalizing image of a bounded whole that appears to be the self yet remains irreconcilable with the bodily experience of uncoordinated movements, partial objects, and chaotic drives. The fluctuating nature of the market, the incompleteness of the information it offers at any particular time, thus becomes the motor of a dynamic relationship. The key thesis that undergirds all of Knorr Cetina's work on flux-objects is this: "we maintain that traders' engagement with markets is based on a match between the self as a sequence of wantings and an unfolding object that provides for these wantings through the lacks it displays." The interconnection of organic and electronic rhythms—the push-pull of greed and market signals—is the basis of postsocial relations. Yet beyond this rhythmic relation of wanting and lack, of unfolding object and inchoate desire, there is always a tantalizing image of the whole: the star trader just one row over, the Hollywood star out on a yacht in the bay, the millionaire exec just returning from China—or the market itself when it suddenly coheres, complete and ravishing, as an opportunity within reach.

For architectural critic Norman Klein, the "scripted spaces" of Las Vegas casinos are the epitome of urban design in financialized culture. Klein homes in on slot machines, which "turned risk into a consumer thrill." They now include screens displaying special effects from the movies, feature realistic showgirls giving players the come-on, and integrate narrative devices from quiz shows and other popular TV series. Yet their major function is statistical control. As Klein observes: "They became the most integrated software network in entertainment, practically a metonym for the globalized electronic economy. They stand in for cybernetic controls across many markets at once. Today, computerized tracking services perform like a bot for the house: tracking players, slots, tables, revenue services, doing the taxes, providing 'up to the minute WIN reporting,' player photos, electronic signature identification, messages for players in their hotel rooms."[13] At the heart of the slots, where the wheels of fortune spin, is a subtle equation whereby the player "senses an internal design" (the math that governs the payback) but also feels "the illusion of luck" (the possibility of a chance event). Profit for the house is ensured through strictly calculated probabilities.

The electronic trading floors that provide a model for contemporary casinos are also theaters of passion subject to integral statistical control. Yet unlike casinos, they are incapable of achieving cybernetic

13 | Norman Klein, *The Vatican to Vegas: A History of Special Effects* (New York: New Press, 2004), p. 340.

closure. The calculus of probabilities is too vast to master, despite the mathematical efforts of quants writing unique equations for personalized over-the-counter derivatives. Storms, earthquakes, meltdowns, and other events continually intervene, at historically unpredictable rates due to the ecological consequences of an overheated global economy. Populations wear down, unable to repay the loans that injected more capital into the system to increase the illusion of luck. Then governments take over with quantitative easing programs that expand the money supply for a further round of the global gamble. As I write, the passionate involvement between traders and the internalized "other" of the market has turned violent: major banks, hedge funds, and ratings agencies collude to threaten the economic stability of the entire European Union, provoking conditions of volatility that offer fresh occasions for high-frequency trading and more obscene profits. The ice-cold cerebral activity of finance takes on the aura of a strangely frenetic sacrificial rite. It's as though the theater of greed and desire had suddenly become a gladiatorial arena. The rest of us—the people in the street—sense that we could be the "other," that is, the victims.

Profane Communication

Separation, for Giorgio Agamben, is the essence of the sacred. It removes objects, places, activities, and people from the world of common usage, transferring them through rite and myth to the sphere of the divine. "Not only is there no religion without separation, but every separation preserves within itself a genuinely religious core."[14] This sacred divide is carried over into the value-form of the commodity, whose abstraction reaches a height in the semiotic universe of the financial markets. But Agamben does not call for any return to genuine religion. The urgency of his thinking is clear in his concept of secularization:

> Secularization is a form of repression. It leaves intact the forces it deals with by simply moving them from one place to another. Thus the political secularization of theological concepts (the transcendence of God as a paradigm of sovereign power) does nothing but displace the heavenly monarchy into an earthly monarchy, leaving its power intact.

All of contemporary capitalism effects a repressive secularization, transforming the absolute divide between priestly and secular status into class hierarchies where economics fully replaces aura. For this reason the grand strategy of Enlightenment, demystification, can no longer apply to the basic operations of power in our societies, which

14 | Giorgio Agamben, "In Praise of Profanation," in *Profanations* (New York: Zone Books, 2007 [orig. 2005]); further quotes are from the same essay. Agamben also develops the notion of profanation in *What Is an Apparatus?* (Stanford University Press, 2009 [orig. 2006]). However, he does not deal with the material and discursive complexity of any specific apparatus, or with any particular acts of profanation.

contain no obscure core of mystery, but only obsessional procedures for the imposition of rationalized myths and rites. In place of secularization, Agamben proposes the act of "profanation": "Both are political operations: the first guarantees the exercise of power by carrying it back to a sacred model; the second deactivates the apparatuses of power and returns to common use the spaces that power had seized."

In societies dominated by the mediatization of two destructive rites—financial crisis and war—the act of profanation becomes necessary to the very existence of democratic politics. By converging on sites of global decision making such as international summits, a previous wave of protesters was able to displace social attention at the very locus where it is concentrated and synchronized with the commands of power. Agamben refers to a kind of defunctionalizing play, which "frees and distracts humanity from the sphere of the sacred, without simply abolishing it." Those were the tactics of the "carnivals against capital" at the century's turn. But at a moment when political control is being ceded to financial traders operating 24/7 through abstractive global networks, the outbreak of embodied dissent on Wall Street and in other financial centers has greater force than the protest carnivals—all the more so because the occupations continue day and night, incarnating another life rather than a disruptive moment. The spillover into the media is tremendous. Once the place of power is altered, its name acquires a different valence: it becomes an invitation to further questioning and defiance, rather than a reminder of disempowerment and cynical manipulation. At issue is a cultural resistance to the depressive effects of scripted society. To describe the nature of profane play, Agamben quotes the linguist Émile Benveniste:

> The power of the sacred act, he writes, lies in the conjunction of the myth that tells the story and the rite that reproduces and stages it. Play breaks up this unity: as *ludus*, or physical play, it drops the myth and preserves the rite; as *iocus*, or wordplay, it effaces the rite and allows the myth to survive. "If the sacred can be defined through the consubstantial unity of myth and rite, we can say that one has play when only half the sacred operation is completed, translating only the myth into words or only the rite into actions."

What could this mean in a secularized context, where myth has been replaced by media, and rite by the instrumentality of mathematical models and computer programs? Consider first of all the most striking emblem of the recent occupations, which is the signage. Oscillating between an endless list of grievances, an angry *J'accuse!*, and a warm invitation to satirical disbelief, these handwritten signs fascinate participants and bystanders, floating above the crowd like headlines from everyday existence. The signs are not yet demands: they are discursive and affective information for the movement itself, clarifying the collective perception of social problems that have been censored from the major media. No less powerful in this regard, despite its purely Web-based appearance, are the letters of people abandoned by the system, the sorrows of the 99 percent that have never made it into any statistic.[15] Wordplay is everywhere at the occupations, substituting direct address and shared invention for the laborious and repressive fabrications of the corporate media. The will to interrupt one-way speech is so strong that even where amplification is available and legal, the occupiers have used the "people's mic" so as to make sure that a speaker's every word can be tested (and tasted) in one's own body before being received as truth. All of this is done in the absence of functional expertise, and of any "demands" whatsoever: the connection between ideological myth and instrumental rite is interrupted. The displacement and release of both direct and mediated speech opens up new faculties of critical intelligence, not only among the protesters on the spot but across the world.

15 | http://wearethe99percent.tumblr.com.

Through the irruption of a social movement, political-economic analysis is returned to common use among the people who are typically on the receiving end. That's fundamental; it's the biggest gain so far. Yet to be effective in breaking the dependence of intellectuals and cultural producers on elite patronage and models of human capital, this expressive intelligence will have to be pushed further into both professional life and everyday practice. There is an irreverence that equalizes, that cuts through privileges and lies; it's the essence of profanity. Like this: a guy at Liberty Square holds a Fox News camera made of cardboard, with a hand-drawn, one-dimensional mic that he thrusts insistently in the face of anyone claiming to be important. The gesture dissolves the repetition-compulsions of the media into pure play: the ethical departure point of profane communication.

A different use of speech is possible when the occupations shatter the narcissistic mirror, mingling bodies, upsetting class and racial divides. This is possible because a major crisis of capitalism brings all kinds of people out into the street. The question is how to go on talking with those you formerly ignored. They could include scientists and technicians who shape behavior through machines, or managers who organize productive collaborations. Normally these people provide services to our rulers. Could they break the connection between instrumental technology and mediated myth?

Engineering, a central concern of communism, was more or less abandoned by the 1968 generation—to disastrous effect, because a movement without *techné* can't convince anyone of its capacity to materially reorganize society. But younger activists have been able to find a new way in, mainly by way of networks. When global computer exchange links are hacked away from the official capitalist ideologies that bind them to the financial apparatus, what results is the open proliferation of a powerful tool. The Global Revolution streaming video network is one example. Among the founders is Vlad Teichberg, who emigrated from Russia to the U.S. when he was ten years old. In an interview with *Democracy Now!* he speaks about the roots of OWS in the Arab Spring and the Spanish Indignado movement. Those who wonder about the struggles of technologists inside the financial apparatus definitely have something to learn from this guy:

> I was a derivatives trader. I was basically working for large banks, betting their money on derivatives products. And my job was understanding how those products work. . . . For me . . . the whole globalization philosophy that was being pushed in the early/mid-nineties, [the idea] that it would be the ultimate equalizer for the world, turned out to be faulty, because of the effect of multinationals. Toward the late nineties I think a lot of people came to the same conclusion: globalization was doing more harm than good. . . . And that's pretty much when I started shifting out of being a supporter of this Ayn Rand approach to looking at the world.[16]

16 | Interview with Vlad Teichberg, www.democracynow.org/2011/11/18/the_revolution_will_be_live_streamed.

A programmer like Teichberg is no longer glued to any established combination of discourse and practice. Refusing hierarchical separations, he's able to divert certain aspects of the financial apparatus toward other ends, to create a planetary network for common use. The failure of neoliberal globalization, which became obvious to him ten years ago, is now a palpable fact for everyone. The potential for a political use of skills that were formerly subordinated to the 1 percent is suddenly enormous. The contradictions of the "new class," absorbed for decades by opportunities in the financialized economy, are returning to the fore. But the only way to keep them alive—and to save them from being captured, channeled, and neutralized—is to use them, not just out on the street but in whatever field you occupy every day. Profanity is only a departure point. The beginning is near, as an OWS slogan has it.

Closing It Down

I started this text in mid-November 2011, with technocrats taking over European states and robocops evicting occupations across the U.S. While British workers pushed for a general strike and Chilean students radicalized their revolt, images of epic street fights poured in from Tahrir Square. Just as Wallerstein had claimed, the "1968 current" was back. It turned out that the same factory—Combined Systems Inc., of Jamestown, Pennsylvania—was supplying tear gas to the American and Egyptian police. On *Al Jazeera* I found a text by William Robinson: "The immense structural inequalities of the global political economy can no longer be contained through consensual mechanisms of social control. The ruling classes have lost legitimacy; we are witnessing a breakdown of ruling-class hegemony on a world scale."[17]

At last it has become obvious that this is a major crisis of capitalism. As in the 1930s and 1970s, it will only be resolved by changing basic parameters of the system. The point is to take part, to generate an agency that can make changes for the better.

It's impressive to learn that as far back as 2007, a financial think tank working for the British military had already understood that under the pressure of crisis, "the middle classes could become a revolutionary class, taking the role envisaged for the proletariat by Marx." Here's what they said:

> The globalization of labor markets and reducing levels of national welfare provision and employment could reduce peoples' attachment to particular states. The growing gap between themselves and a small number of highly visible super-rich individuals might fuel disillusion with meritocracy, while the growing urban under-classes are likely to pose an increasing threat to social order and stability, as the burden of acquired debt and the failure of pension provision begins to bite. Faced by these twin challenges, the world's middle-classes might unite, using access to knowledge, resources and skills to shape transnational processes in their own class interest.[18]

Can intellectuals and cultural producers of the North, acting in parallel to their peers in the South, contribute to a movement of resistance against inequality and oppression on the scale of the world-revolution of 1968? Can we use the solidarities brought by economic crisis to substantially transform the current hegemony? Can we intervene in a new way, to provoke not a violent reaction, but instead a positive structural change in the repressive course of what is currently being called "necropolitics"?[19]

Revolts in North America and Europe will never be articulated in the same way as those in countries such as Egypt or Tunisia, for reasons of persistent geopolitical inequality in particular. But the secret link of our crisscrossing histories is that ultimately we share the same opponents. Behind the desiring-machine of the financial markets, the authority of the generals lies in wait. It was obvious throughout the past decade, when the dot-com bust was followed by global security panic and two brutal wars; but the course of everyday life went on unperturbed, in a period of massive complicity between the middle classes and our rapacious elites. The point is to tear away from the imperatives of the 1 percent that have reshaped public institutions and penetrated the cultural-intellectual sphere so deeply. This requires playing a different game, no longer a gamble. Without tangible proof of a change of loyalties—achieved essentially by means of projects constructed outside the professional economy—there is no way to

17 | William I. Robinson, "Global Rebellion: The Coming Chaos?," *Al Jazeera English*, www.aljazeera.com/indepth/opinion/2011/11/20111130121556567265.html.

18 | "The DCDC Global Strategic Trends Programme, 2007–2036," www.frequencyclear.tv/strat_trends.pdf.

19 | Achille Mbembe, "Necropolitics," *Public Culture* 15, no. 1 (2003), http://www.jhfc.duke.edu/icuss/pdfs/Mbembe.pdf.

gain the trust of others. Without the capacity to reach into established fields and workplaces—achieved essentially by a courageous defense of philosophical principles against the current rules—there is no way to gain the capacities of social transformation.

Similar dilemmas have already confronted the growing professional-managerial classes of the South. One finds an important insight in the chronicles of Mark LeVine, a young University of California prof who has been on the scene in Egypt. Recounting a midnight visit to Tahrir, he discusses the desire of the movement's informal "leaders" to create a space directly on the square for the poetry, music, cinema, and other cultural forms that have sustained the revolt since its beginnings:

> In other words, the leaders of Tahrir want to institutionalize the incredible creativity of the revolution, from musical performances and film to artwork, poetry and story-telling. These activities have sustained protesters during the darkest days of violence and have helped to attract hundreds of thousands of "ordinary Egyptians" to the Meidan during each of the occupations since January. This would constitute a permanent counterpoint to the state media and other mechanisms that the government and elite have at their disposal, through which they try to convince Egyptians that the Tahriris are little more than "thugs" who don't have their interests at heart.[20]

20 | Mark LeVine, "Tahrir's Late Night Conversations," *Al Jazeera English*, www.aljazeera.com/indepth/opinion/2011/12/20 1112511219971906.html.

All Internet sites accessed on December 15, 2011.

In the corrupt and declining countries of the North, artists and intellectuals need to rediscover this desire for a culture outside the financialized state—a profane culture that is powerful, sophisticated, and deep but open to common use. Only in this way can we strengthen the affects of resistance and build the capacity to create alternatives. And there is no time left for ambivalence. A structural crisis can only be resolved by major transformations, for better or for worse. Social movements inevitably intervene, but often with unwanted consequences, as became obvious in the Nixon years. The challenge today, in societies dominated by the aging and fearful rich, is to hold off police violence while pushing defiantly for economic and ecological transformation. At some point over the next few years it will likely require decisive action, like those days when the people of the former East went out into the streets and did not leave. But we will not get there by just hoping—because if financial chaos really hits, the generals have a plan.

Class strategies are formed by the aggregation of small decisions. Ask yourself, ask those around you, what it will take for *us* to close the casino.

This text was developed for a self-organized seminar entitled "Three Crises: 30s—70s—Today." The archive of the entire seminar is available at http://messhall.org.

Brian Holmes is a cultural critic and autonomous researcher, living in Chicago.

Brian Holmes
Das Profane und die Finanzmärkte. Eine Gebrauchsanleitung zur Schließung des Casinos

Ich will nicht mit einem Fluch beginnen, sondern mit einer sehr schönen Annäherung, die allgemein für real gehalten wird, für Millionen von Menschen jedoch geheimnisumwittert ist. Ich spreche von der »Bewegung der Plätze«, die sich beiderseits der Kluft zwischen Norden und Süden ausbreitet. Was ist das verborgene Bindeglied zwischen den Bewegungen der Mittelschicht und des Prekariats gegen die Diktate des Finanzkapitals – Occupy Wall Street und die europäischen »Empörten« – und den weitaus gefährlicheren Bemühungen, die Diktaturen in Nordafrika und im Nahen Osten zu beenden? Auf welche Verbindung zwischen den Regionen, in denen sich der globale Reichtum konzentriert, und jenen, aus denen unablässig Arbeitskräfte, Ressourcen und Zinszahlungen abgezogen werden, könnte man womöglich schließen?

Immanuel Wallerstein behauptet, dass sich in den Aufständen im Nahen Osten und in Nordafrika zwei historische Gruppen miteinander messen. Die eine, die er als »1968er-Bewegung« (1968 current) bezeichnet, setzt sich aus gewaltlosen, direktdemokratischen Graswurzelbewegungen zusammen, die im Namen einer Gleichheit, die den Respekt für grundlegende Unterschiede einschließt, alle Formen von Exklusion und Machtmissbrauch infrage stellen. Die andere Gruppe besteht aus Menschen, die gegen solche Bewegungen opponieren und auf jede erdenkliche Weise danach streben, sie zu vereinnahmen, einzudämmen und zu neutralisieren – und dies sind in Nordafrika und im Nahen Osten in erster Linie die Vertreter der reichen Ölindustrie und von den USA unterstützte Diktatoren. Für Wallerstein sind die derzeitigen Aufstände, nach einer jahrzehntelangen Latenzphase, eine Fortsetzung der »Weltrevolution von 1968«, die aus seiner Sicht von 1966 bis 1970 dauerte.[1]

Wenn dies zutrifft, teilen die Menschen, die heute auf die Straße gehen, immerhin eine Geschichte. Denn die Weltrevolution von 1968 fand auch in Europa und in den Vereinigten Staaten statt, wo sie sich entscheidend um die Solidarität und die direkte Kooperation zwischen Studenten und Intellektuellen der Mittelschicht im Norden und den unterdrückten Menschen im Süden drehte – was in den USA nicht nur Vietnam und Lateinamerika hieß, sondern auch den Süden unseres eigenen Landes umfasste. Weiße gingen nach Alabama, Georgia und Mississippi, um mit der Bürgerrechtsbewegung zusammenzuarbeiten. Unterdrückte Minderheiten, vor allem die Black Panthers, lasen Frantz Fanon und andere antikolonialistische Denker und bezeichneten sich selbst als Völker der Dritten Welt. Die Neue Linke versuchte, ihre Unterstützung für die vietnamesischen Revolutionäre zum Ausdruck zu bringen, indem sie »den Krieg nach Hause holte«. Die »68er-Bewegung« war von dem gewaltigen, aufrührerischen und oftmals gescheiterten Experiment einer Klassen- und Staatengrenzen überschreitenden Kooperation gekennzeichnet. Doch reicht diese historische Erinnerung, um die Konzentration von direktdemokratischen Praktiken innerhalb der Bewegung der Plätze zu erklären?

Wohl kaum. Um unsere komplexeren gemeinsamen Grundlagen zu entdecken, müssen wir auf die reaktionäre Gegenbewegung zurückblicken, die auf 1968 folgte und schließlich im Neoliberalismus mündete. In den USA begann sie mit der Wahl von Richard Nixon. Er stand für ein Law-and-Order-Programm, und seine Regierung unterdrückte durch Geheimdienstoperationen inländische Regierungskritiker, beschloss Gesetze für Programme zur »räumlichen Dekonzentration« zugunsten einer innerstädtischen Gentrifizierung, erfand SWAT (special weapons and tactics)-Teams für Angriffe auf die Ghettos, begründete den gefängnisindustriellen Komplex und bot Pinochets Militärregime in Chile Unterstützung an, was letztlich einer koordinierten Unterdrückung der lateinamerikanischen Linken durch

1 | Immanuel Wallerstein, »The Contradictions of the Arab Spring«, auf: *Al Jazeera English*, www.aljazeera.com/indepth/opinion/2011/11/20111111101711539134.html.

die Operation Condor seit Mitte der 1970er Jahre Vorschub leistete. Überdies fielen die Friedensverhandlungen des Jom-Kippur-Kriegs 1973 und das OPEC-Embargo in seine Amtszeit. Dies führte einerseits zur amerikanischen Stabilisierung Ägyptens (durch Militärhilfen, die 1979 im Rahmen des Abkommens von Camp David offiziell gemacht wurden) und andererseits zu den neuen Ölpreisen und der Einführung eines Kapitalkreislaufs, der westliche Banken, Maschinenbauunternehmen und Rüstungsproduzenten mit den repressivsten Erdöl exportierenden Regimes verband. Der gesamte Prozess zementierte die Position autoritärer Führer in der arabischen Welt und lieferte das Geld für eine ganze Reihe ruinöser Darlehen an Entwicklungsländer in aller Welt. Die jüngst in Nordafrika und im Nahen Osten gestürzten Diktatoren stammen aus dieser Zeit. Somit erlebten die 1970er Jahre die Einsetzung einer polizeilichen und militärischen Ordnung, die im In- und Ausland danach strebte – und das tut sie noch immer –, die »68er-Bewegung« zu vereinnahmen und einzudämmen.

Da sich die Polizei im Norden zunehmend militarisiert, wird auch die Erfahrung von Unterdrückung zu etwas, das die heutigen Bewegungen – wie gewohnt auf unterschiedliche Weise – miteinander teilen. Doch auch dies ist wieder nicht die ganze Geschichte, und so muss ein weiterer historischer Moment in den Blick genommen werden. In den USA und allen anderen entwickelten Ländern schienen die Studentenproteste und die Entstehung einer Gegenkultur den Aufstieg einer »neuen Klasse« anzukündigen, die fähig war, in immer bürokratischeren Systemen an die Schalthebel der Macht zu gelangen. Diese »neue Klasse« bestand aus Verwaltern, Wissenschaftlern, Ingenieuren, Pädagogen, Sozialarbeitern, Meinungsmachern und Künstlern.[2] Sie wurde zu einer Zeit, in der sich die Regierungsfunktionen dramatisch ausweiteten und die alten Patrizier zurückblieben, an den liberalen Universitäten des Wohlfahrtsstaats ausgebildet. An die Stelle der Führerschaft »bedeutender Männer« traten die Entscheidungen von Kommissionen, und der Privatbesitz von Unternehmen galt zunehmend als juristische Fiktion.[3] In den Augen der Neokonservativen drohte die Studentenrevolte, den bereits existierenden Mainstream-Trend zu einer kollektiven Kontrolle der amerikanischen politischen Ökonomie zu radikalisieren. Die gesellschaftlichen Kämpfe der 1970er Jahre, inmitten einer tiefen Wirtschaftskrise, drehten sich darum, diese mögliche Machtübernahme zu fördern oder zu blockieren.

Jüngere soziologische Untersuchungen stellen fest, dass es einem reformierten und transformierten kapitalistischen System nach einer Periode weit verbreiteter Entfremdung, die mit jeder bedeutenden Krise einhergeht, gelingen muss, sein ausgewiesenes leitendes und technisches Personal, zusammen mit den künstlerischen und intellektuellen Kulturproduzenten, erneut zu integrieren.[4] Die neue

2 | Innerhalb eines Jahres erschienen drei Bücher über diese neue Klasse: Pat Walker (Hrsg.), *Between Labor and Capital*, Boston: South End Press 1979; A. W. Gouldner, *The Future of Intellectuals and the Rise of the New Class*, New York: Seabury 1979; und B. Bruce-Briggs (Hrsg.), *The New Class?*, New Brunswick: Transaction Books 1979. Im ersten Buch findet sich der Wiederabdruck eines wichtigen Essays von Barbara und John Ehrenreich über »The Professional-Managerial Class«, das dritte enthält neokonservative Standpunkte.

3 | Zu Fragen von Eigentum und Kontrolle siehe A. A. Berle und G. C. Means, *The Modern Corporation and Private Property*, New York: Harcourt, Brace and World 1968 [Orig. 1932]; James Burnham, *The Managerial Revolution*, New York: John Day 1941 (dt. *Das Regime der Manager*, Stuttgart: Union Deutsche Verlagsgesellschaft 1941); J. K. Galbraith, *The New Industrial State*, Boston: Houghton Mifflin 1967 (dt. *Die moderne Industriegesellschaft*, München: Droemer Knaur 1970–1974).

4 | Siehe Luc Boltanski und Eve Chiapello, *Der neue Geist des Kapitalismus*, Konstanz: UVK Universitätsverlag Konstanz 2003 [Orig. 1999], sowie meinen Text »The Flexible Personality« (2002), http://eipcp.net/transversal/1106/holmes/en.

Ordnung muss das Vertrauen derer zurückgewinnen, die damit beauftragt werden, ihre Logik anzuwenden und zu reproduzieren. Wie wurde dies hinsichtlich der Managerklassen Nordamerikas und Europas sowie durchaus ähnlicher Schichten in den Entwicklungsländern von den 1980er Jahren bis heute erreicht? Die Beantwortung dieser Frage wird sowohl eine eklatante Kluft als auch die verborgenen Beziehungen zwischen den Bewegungen des Nordens und Südens aufdecken.

Meine These dazu lautet wie folgt: Die Integration der Managerklassen in die neoliberale Phase des Kapitalismus vollzog sich durch einen komplexen, aber einheitlichen Mechanismus, den man als Finanzdispositiv bezeichnen könnte. Man könnte aber auch einfach Casino dazu sagen. Seine Abläufe machen sich im gesamten gesellschaftlichen Spektrum bemerkbar, nicht nur im Geschäftsleben, sondern auch in der Kunst, im Bildungswesen, in der öffentlichen Verwaltung, in Technik, Medien, Urbanismus, Diplomatie und am stärksten in der Sozialpsychologie. Die notwendige Kehrseite einer systematischen militärischen Unterdrückung ist ein adrenalingeladenes elektronisches Würfelspiel. Wenn wir die Wall Street in der globalen Hauptstadt des Kapitals New York City oder ein anderes Bankenviertel in einer anderen Stadt besetzen, opponieren wir gegen die integrative Strategie jener, die versuchen, die Auswirkungen der Weltrevolution zu vereinnahmen, einzudämmen und zu neutralisieren. Auf diese Weise solidarisieren wir uns mit unseren Brüdern und Schwestern in Nordafrika und im Nahen Osten (sowie in Lateinamerika und anderswo) durch Maßnahmen, die mit ihren keineswegs identisch sind, sondern parallel zu diesen verlaufen. Könnte man die Grenze zur direkten Zusammenarbeit überschreiten? Diese Frage wird uns noch eine Weile beschäftigen.

Die globale Wette

Marxisten wie David Harvey interpretieren den »Financial Turn«, der Anfang der 1970er Jahre einsetzte, als eine »Klassenstrategie«, um die Vorrechte des Eigentums wiederherzustellen, wodurch in unserer Zeit die weltweiten ein Prozent an die Macht gelangten.[5] Andere, wie Michael Hudson oder der 2009 verstorbene Peter Gowan, konzentrieren sich auf die Strategien des amerikanischen Staats: Die strukturelle Unterstützung der neoliberalen Finanzwirtschaft ist Washingtons »globale Wette«, um die Kontrolle über das internationale Währungssystem zu behalten.[6] Gérard Duménil und Dominique Lévy verbinden beide Herangehensweisen miteinander, führen jedoch zugleich

5 | David Harvey, *Kleine Geschichte des Neoliberalismus*, Zürich: Rotpunktverlag 2007 [Orig. 2005].

6 | Michael Hudson, *Super Imperialism*, London: Pluto Press 2003 [Orig. 1972]; Peter Gowan, *The Global Gamble*, London: Verso 1999.

einen entscheidenden Klassenbegriff ein. Aus ihrer Sicht stellte der keynesianische Fordismus einen Kompromiss zwischen Mittel- und Arbeiterklasse dar, während Erstere unter dem Neoliberalismus (oder dem, was ich als Neoliberalen Informationalismus bezeichne) erneut in den Dienst des Kapitals gezogen wurde.[7] In der Kunstwelt wird dies durch die Vervielfachung von milliardenschweren Mäzenen und Firmenmuseen nur zu deutlich. Doch betrachten wir lieber eine Figur, die eher dem Mainstream dieses Klassenkompromisses zuzurechnen ist: den Finanzmakler, der im niedrigsten Rang des »Golden Boy« auf einen Schlag sagenhaft reich werden oder alles verlieren, in jungen Jahren ausbrennen und grenzenlos scheitern kann.

Der Trader einer großen Bank oder eines bedeutenden Hedgefonds, den Blick starr auf eine individuell angeordnete Reihe von Bildschirmen gerichtet, wird in ein transnationales Netzwerk hineingezogen, das aus Zehntausenden von Institutionen und Millionen einzelner Akteure besteht. Er arbeitet mit Aktien, Bonds und Währungen sowie zunehmend mit Derivaten dieser zugrundeliegenden Werte, die durch die Anwendung mathematischer Formeln entstehen. Seine Aktivität verortet ihn an der Kreuzung zweier widersprüchlicher Theorien.

Auf der einen Seite ist er mit Strömen von Primärdaten konfrontiert, die für vollkommen objektiv gehalten werden. Es sind Preise, Marktfakten, generiert von anonymen Käufern und Verkäufern, deren kollektivem Urteil man unterstellt, dass es reale Informationen über Waren und Dienstleistungen liefere. Der Handel agiert, um kleinere Preisunterschiede durch das Verfahren der »Arbitrage« zu glätten, indem man etwas an einem Ort etwas billiger kauft und an einem anderen Ort etwas teurer verkauft. Auf diese Weise werden Ungenauigkeiten vermeintlich korrigiert, das System wird vervollkommnet. Die Vorstellung, dass Marktpreise ein perfektes Gleichgewicht zwischen Angebot und Nachfrage gewährleisten und nur eine letztlich zufällige restliche Fluktuation hinterlassen, ist unter dem Begriff »Effizienzmarkthypothese« geläufig.[8] Sie garantiert den dauerhaften Glauben an die Neutralität der Finanzspekulation.

Gleichzeitig wird der Trader als Ausnahmeerscheinung, Einzelgänger und Genie gefeiert. Er verfügt über einzigartiges Wissen, blitzartige Schnelligkeit, unvergleichliche Aggressivität und ein unheimliches »Gespür« für Trends. Durch seine Verarbeitung von Informationen, die theoretisch jedermann zugänglich sind, schafft der Trader ständig Werte für die Bank und ihre Kunden. Er tut dies in der strengsten Abgetrenntheit vom Schicksal realer Güter oder Dienstleistungen, da er Geld aus Zahlen machen kann, die wahlweise steigen oder fallen. Er unterhält seine eigene Buchführung von Gewinnen und Verlusten, und obwohl er mit dem Geld anderer Leute hantiert, muss er außergewöhnliche und originelle Entscheidungen treffen,

7 | Gérard Duménil und Dominique Lévy, *The Crisis of Neoliberalism*, Cambridge, Mass.: Harvard University Press 2011, bes. Kap. 1 und 5.

8 | Justin Fox, *The Myth of the Rational Market*, New York: HarperCollins 2009.

da er dafür bezahlt wird, nur jene besonderen Risiken einzugehen, durch die er einen Gewinn erzielen kann. Der Trader ist durch etwas definiert, das die ökonomische Theorie für unmöglich hält: durch die Fähigkeit, »gegen die Bank zu gewinnen«. Hyperwettbewerb und virtuose Geschicklichkeit machen ihn zum Mittelschichtshelden des Neoliberalen Informationalismus.

Wie kann eine eng gefasste Klassenstrategie, die sich auf bestimmte Personen und technische Funktionen konzentriert, auf eine gesamte Epoche übergreifen und auf ein ganzes diffuses Zeitalter des menschlichen Zusammenlebens abfärben? Michel Foucault formulierte 1977 in einem Interview eine Definition eines seiner Schlüsselbegriffe: das Dispositiv. Trotz ihres hohen Abstraktionsgrades liest sich seine Erörterung wie die Zeichenerklärung eines Kartografen unserer finanzialisierten Gesellschaft. Das Dispositiv ist ein »Bündel von Beziehungen«, das eine Reihe scheinbar unzusammenhängender Elemente miteinander verknüpft: »ein entschieden heterogenes Ensemble, das Diskurse, Institutionen, architekturale Einrichtungen, reglementierende Entscheidungen, Gesetze, administrative Maßnahmen, wissenschaftliche Aussagen, philosophische, moralische oder philanthropische Lehrsätze [...] umfaßt.« Es ist eine »Formation, deren Hauptfunktion zu einem gegebenen historischen Zeitpunkt darin bestanden hat, auf einen Notstand (urgence) zu antworten.« Doch jenseits dieses Notstands konstituiert sich das Dispositiv als »Ort eines doppelten Prozesses [...]: Prozeß einerseits einer funktionellen Überdeterminierung« und »Prozeß einer ständigen strategischen Wiederauffüllung andererseits«. Schließlich merkt Foucault an: »Um sagen zu können: dies ist ein Dispositiv, suche ich danach, welches die Elemente gewesen sind, die in eine Rationalität, eine gegebene Übereinkunft [*une concertation donnée*] eingegangen sind.«[9] Das Ziel besteht darin, die Wirkungsweisen einer herrschenden Vorstellung anhand einer ineinandergreifenden Reihe gesellschaftlicher Formen zu begreifen.

Nach einer anfänglichen Untersuchung jener Disziplinierungseinrichtung, die als Panoptikum bekannt ist, richtete Foucault seine Aufmerksamkeit auf die »Sicherheitsdispositive«, die für eine liberale oder Laissez-faire-Wirtschaftspolitik charakteristisch sind. Sein erstes Beispiel war ein Entwurf für die Stadtsanierung von Nantes aus dem 18. Jahrhundert, der unter anderem vorsah, neue Straßenzüge anzulegen, die vier sich überschneidende Funktionen erfüllen sollten: die Durchlüftung von Gegenden mit hygienischen Missständen, die Erleichterung des Handels innerhalb der Stadt, den direkten Anschluss an überregionale Verkehrsnetze sowie die Verkehrsüberwachung in einem städtischen Umfeld, das nicht länger von Mauern umgeben war und in dem es keine Sperrstunde mehr gab. Der Plan entwirft keine geschlossenen und für ausschließliche Ver-

9 | Michel Foucault, »Ein Spiel um die Psychoanalyse. Gespräch mit Angehörigen des Département der Psychoanalyse der Universität Paris VIII in Vincennes« [Orig. 1977], übers. v. Monika Metzeger, in: *Dispositive der Macht. Michel Foucault. Über Sexualität, Wissen und Wahrheit*, Berlin: Merve 1978, S. 118–175.

wendungszwecke definierten Räume wie in einem disziplinarischen Schema, sondern schafft eine Reihe multifunktionaler Korridore, die sich – gemäß den Strukturen eines nicht ganz vorhersagbaren zukünftigen Wachstums – in mehrere Richtungen ausdehnen können. Gouvernementalität arbeitet nach den Gesetzen der Wahrscheinlichkeit, weniger als einzelner Befehl, sondern eher als ein System, das Zirkulation ermöglicht.

Die Wirkung des Sicherheitsdispositivs besteht darin, niemandem etwas aufzuzwingen, sondern stattdessen aus den spontanen Verhaltensweisen einer bestimmten Bevölkerung die günstigsten Elemente auszuwählen und eine Umgebung dann so zu gestalten, dass sich diese weiter optimieren lassen, bis ihr Vorherrschen unerwünschte Merkmale ausschließt. Die Idee besteht darin, »diese verschiedenen Normalitätsaufteilungen wechselseitig in Gang zu setzen und auf diese Weise zu bewirken, daß die ungünstigsten auf die günstigsten zurückgeführt werden«.[10] Es gibt auch weiterhin eine unverhohlene Unterdrückung, doch diese ist den »gefährlichen« Elementen vorbehalten, die das System durcheinanderbringen könnten. Während der zurückliegenden drei Jahrzehnte prägte eben dieses Schema die bevorzugten Beziehungen zwischen den Besitzern konzentrierten Kapitals und ihren Dienern, den Managerklassen.

Wenn Foucault den Spekulationsboom der späten 1980er Jahre noch miterlebt hätte, hätte er im transnationalen Finanzwesen das zentrale Sicherheitsdispositiv des neoliberalen Zeitalters erkannt. Der Computerhandel wendet die Logik der Risikooptimierung auf die Zirkulation der Kapitalströme an, und zwar innerhalb genau definierter technologischer, informationeller und juristischer Umfelder. Sehen wir uns an, wie diese Umfelder nach dem Zusammenbruch des Bretton-Woods-Systems fester Wechselkurse 1973 entstanden sind. Devisenterminkontrakte, Optionen und andere Derivate reagierten auf die dringende Anforderung, transnationale Geschäftsvorgänge unter den Bedingungen einer beispiellosen Volatilität zu managen, wo Werte stündlich schwankten und Preise vielfältigen Risiken unterworfen waren. In Kombination mit vernetzten Preisinformationssystemen trugen ausgeklügelte mathematische Modelle nicht nur dazu bei, diese Risiken durch komlexe Hedging-Strategien zu verkleinern; sie dienten auch dazu, in einer Zeit, in der Unternehmen eine globale Ebene erreichten, die Liquidität für eine Welle von Fusionen und Übernahmen zu generieren. Doch der Financial Turn passt auch in eine umfassendere Strategie zur Reintegration der Managerklassen, deren jüngeres Personal durch die Standardisierung und Reglementierung des Fordismus entfremdet worden war.

Diese Strategie beruhte auf der Anerkennung der Tatsache, dass individuelle Differenz konstitutiv für ein Humankapital ist, dem

10 | Michel Foucault, »Vorlesung 3 (Sitzung vom 25. Januar 1978)«, in: Ders., *Geschichte der Gouvernementalität I. Sicherheit, Territorium, Bevölkerung. Vorlesung am Collège de France 1977–1978*, hrsg. v. Michel Sennelart, übers. v. Claudia Brede-Konersmann und Jürgen Schröder, Frankfurt a. M.: Suhrkamp 2004 [Orig. 2004], S. 87–133, hier S. 98.

zum Ausgleich für die Abschaffung öffentlicher Einrichtungen und Leistungsansprüche eine entsprechende »Rendite« in Aussicht gestellt werden sollte. Die Finanzkrise des Sozialstaats könne gelöst werden, wenn man alle Ausgaben für die soziale Reproduktion – Gesundheit, Bildung, Transport, Wohnen, Arbeitslosigkeit, Ruhestand – den Einzelnen als Investitionen in ihr Humankapital zukommen ließe; hierfür könnten private Banken Kredite gegen Zinsen zur Verfügung stellen. Die Angehörigen der »neuen Klasse« standen nicht mehr so sehr unter dem Einfluss von Ideologie, Patriotismus und den Werten von Ehe und Familie; vielmehr bot die verlockende Aussicht auf den Zugang zu einem gewissen Spekulationskapital, in Verbindung mit den monatlichen Ratenzahlungen von Studienkrediten und Hypotheken- oder Verbraucherdarlehen, präzisere Möglichkeiten der Verhaltenskontrolle.

Während sich die Universitäten darauf einstellten, der Bildungswirtschaft zu dienen, wurden die populärsten Künstler und Intellektuellen zu Kultur-Stars, und einige Wissenschaftler begannen, aus geistigem Eigentum bedeutende Gewinne zu erzielen. Und am oberen Ende des gesellschaftlichen Spektrums wurden Eigentumsvorrechte wiederhergestellt, als der Shareholder-Value zum unternehmerischen Leitprinzip aufstieg. Anstatt sich auf die Produktion zu konzentrieren, verfolgten Konzerne nun ein einziges Ziel: für ihre Eigentümer Geld und damit gesellschaftliche Macht zu generieren.

Dies sind enorme Veränderungen gegenüber dem keynesianischen Fordismus. Doch man könnte noch weiter gehen und aufzeigen, wie die kybernetische Rechenart des Finanzwesens als koordinierende Rationalität für Just-in-time-Produktion und Vertrieb fungiert. Wenn die Finanzminister der G-20 danach streben, einer transnationalen Kreditklemme vorzubeugen, dienen sie eben diesem Just-in-time-System. Die Rhythmen des Finanzwesens beherrschen mittlerweile das gesamte Zirkulationssystem der Weltwirtschaft.[11] Wenn wir jedoch verstehen wollen, wie die sozialen Beziehungen des Börsenparketts – durch eine »funktionelle Überdetermination« des Finanzdispositivs – auf die gesamte heutige Kultur übergegriffen und diese umgestaltet haben, werden wir auf die Mikroebene zurückkehren und uns genauer ansehen müssen, was im Casino wirklich vor sich geht.

11 | Siehe meinen Artikel »Do Containers Dream of Electric People? The Social Form of Just-in-Time Production«, in: *Open*, Nr. 21, 2011: »Im/mobility«, www.skor.nl/_files/Files/OPEN21EN_P30-44.pdf.

Starfuckers

Die scharfsinnigsten Beobachtungen hierzu stammen aus der Feldforschung, die Karin Knorr Cetina und Urs Bruegger in einem Team von Währungshändlern der UBS in Zürich durchgeführt haben. Sie behaupten, dort eine »postsoziale Beziehung« entdeckt zu haben: eine intellektuelle, perzeptuelle und viszerale Interaktion mit dem »Markt auf dem Bildschirm«, den die Händler als »einen komplexen ›Anderen‹ [erleben], zu dem sie in einer engen, ja sogar obsessiven Beziehung stehen«.[12] Den beiden Soziologen zufolge ist der Markt, der sich auf den Bildschirmen zu einer Präsenz zusammenfügt, ständig fluktuiert und sich in undefinierbarer Art und Weise immer wieder wandelt, nicht von einer »Lebensform« zu unterscheiden. Seine Komplexität beruht auf einem doppelten Aspekt, denn er ist ein Strom, in den man eintaucht und den man verändert, und zugleich ein quasi bewusster Anderer, dem man mit dem Schock des Wiedererkennens begegnet. Wie Bruegger und Knorr Cetina schreiben, bedeutete »die Übertragung des Markts auf den Bildschirm […], dass Händler nun in der Lage sind, sich im Markt zu positionieren, indem sie in seinen sich überlagernden Netzwerken zu Akteuren werden, und sich gleichzeitig auf den Markt auf dem Bildschirm wie auf einen externalisierten Anderen zu beziehen, eine Art überlegenes Wesen, das alle Transaktionen beobachtet und ihre kontextuellen Bedingungen und Motivationen umfasst.« Die Interaktion mit dem Markt ist stürmisch und leidenschaftlich und schwankt zwischen dem Verlangen und der Angst vor Schwankungen, der narzisstischen Euphorie des Gewinns und dem brutalen Schock des Verlusts. Misserfolg wird in anschaulichen Metaphern ausgedrückt, in denen der Händler den sexualisierten Aggressionen des Marktes ausgesetzt ist: »I got shafted, I got bent over, I got blown up, I got raped, I got stuffed/the guy stuffed me, I got fucked, I got hammered, I got killed.« Man bedenke, dass sich all dies am Arbeitsplatz, mit einem scheinbar kühlen und technokratischen Blick auf drei oder sechs oder acht Computerbildschirme, abspielt.

Die beiden Autoren vergleichen, unter Verweis auf den Aufsatz des Psychoanalytikers Jacques Lacan über das »Spiegelstadium« der menschlichen Entwicklung, diese Beziehung zum Markt auf dem Bildschirm mit der Beziehung des Kleinkinds zu seinem Spiegelbild; dieses wird als das faszinierende Bild eines umgrenzten Ganzen erlebt, das als Selbst erscheint, jedoch mit der körperlichen Erfahrung von unkoordinierten Bewegungen, Partialobjekten und chaotischen Trieben unvereinbar bleibt. So werden der schwankende Charakter des Markts und die Unvollständigkeit der Informationen, die er zu einem bestimmten Zeitpunkt bietet, zum Motor einer dynamischen Beziehung. Die Hauptthese, die sämtlichen Arbeiten Knorr Cetinas zu prozesshaften Objekten zugrunde liegt, lautet: »[W]ir behaupten, dass die Beziehungen von Händlern zu den Märkten auf einem Spiel zwischen dem Selbst als einer Reihe von Wünschen und einem prozesshaften Objekt beruht, das diese Wünsche durch die ihm innewoh-

12 | Karin Knorr Cetina und Urs Bruegger, »Traders' Engagement with Markets: A Postsocial Relationship«, in: *Theory, Culture & Society*, Nr. 19, Dezember 2002. Alle Zitate in diesem und dem folgenden Absatz stammen aus diesem Artikel.

nenden Mängel hervorruft.« Diese Verbindung von organischen und elektronischen Rhythmen – der Takt der Gier und der Signale des Marktes – bildet die Grundlage postsozialer Beziehungen. Doch über dieser rhythmischen Beziehung zwischen Wunsch und Mangel, zwischen dem prozesshaften Objekt und dem aufsteigenden Begehren, steht immer das verlockende Bild des Ganzen: der Börsen-Star eine Reihe weiter, der Hollywood-Star auf einer Yacht in der Bucht, der millionenschwere Manager, der gerade aus China zurückkommt – oder der Markt selbst, wenn er plötzlich als greifbare Chance eine vollständige, atemberaubende Einheit bildet.

Für den Architekturkritiker Norman Klein sind die narrativ gestalteten »scripted spaces« der Casinos von Las Vegas der Inbegriff von Stadtplanung in einer finanzialisierten Kultur. Klein zielt besonders auf die Glücksspielautomaten ab, die »das Risiko in einen konsumierbaren Nervenkitzel verwandelt haben«. Sie verfügen mittlerweile über Bildschirme mit kinematografischen Spezialeffekten, präsentieren realistische Showgirls, die die Spieler ködern, und verwenden erzählerische Elemente aus Quizsendungen und anderen beliebten Fernsehserien. Ihre wichtigste Funktion ist jedoch die statistische Kontrolle. Wie Klein feststellt, wurden sie »zur bestintegrierten Entwicklungsumgebung im Unterhaltungsgeschäft, fast eine Metonymie der globalisierten elektronischen Ökonomie. Sie stehen für die simultane kybernetische Kontrolle über mehrere Märkte. Heute fungieren computergestützte Tracking-Services für die Spielbank wie eine Suchmaschine: Sie verfolgen Spieler, Spielautomaten, Tische, Finanzverwaltung und Steuererklärung, liefern ›minutenaktuelle Gewinnberichte‹, Fotos von Spielern, elektronische Unterschriftenidentifikation und Nachrichten an die Spieler in ihren Hotelzimmern«.[13] Im Innersten der Spielautomaten, wo sich die Glücksräder drehen, gibt es eine subtile Gleichung, durch die der Spieler »eine innere Struktur wahrnimmt« (die Mathematik, die die Rückzahlungen reguliert) und gleichzeitig »die Illusion von Glück« (die Möglichkeit eines Zufallsereignisses) verspürt. Der Gewinn für die Bank ist aufgrund streng kalkulierter Wahrscheinlichkeiten garantiert.

Der elektronische Börsenhandel, der den heutigen Spielcasinos als Vorbild dient, ist zugleich ein Theater der Leidenschaft, das einer umfassenden statistischen Kontrolle unterworfen ist. Im Unterschied zu den Casinos ist er allerdings nicht in der Lage, operationale Geschlossenheit zu erreichen. Die Wahrscheinlichkeitsrechnung ist – trotz der mathematischen Anstrengungen quantitativer Fondsmanager, die einzigartige Programme für individuelle, direkt gehandelte Derivate schreiben – zu gigantisch, als dass man sie beherrschen könnte. Infolge der ökologischen Auswirkungen einer überhitzten Weltwirtschaft treten in historisch nicht vorhersagbarer Geschwindig-

13 | Norman Klein, *The Vatican to Vegas: A History of Special Effects*, New York: New Press 2004, S. 340.

keit immer wieder Ereignisse wie Stürme, Erdbeben und Kernschmelzen ein. Die Bevölkerungen werden zermürbt und sind nicht mehr in der Lage, die Kredite zurückzuzahlen, die mehr Kapital in das System gepumpt haben, um die Illusion des Glücks zu vergrößern. Dann intervenieren die Regierungen mit einer quantitativen Lockerung, die die Geldmenge für eine weitere Runde der globalen Wette vergrößert. Während ich dies schreibe, werden die leidenschaftlichen Beziehungen zwischen den Händlern und dem internalisierten »Anderen« des Marktes gewalttätig: Große Banken, Hedgefonds und Rating-Agenturen arbeiten zusammen, um die wirtschaftliche Stabilität des gesamten europäischen Kontinents zu bedrohen und damit jene Volatilität auszulösen, die neue Gelegenheiten für Hochfrequenz-Handel und noch mehr obszöne Gewinne bietet. Die eiskalte zerebrale Aktivität des Finanzwesens nimmt die Aura eines seltsam frenetischen Opferrituals an. Es scheint, als habe sich das Theater der Gier und des Begehrens plötzlich in eine Gladiatorenarena verwandelt. Der Rest von uns – die Leute auf der Straße – stellt fest, dass wir die »Anderen« sein könnten, also die Opfer.

14 | Giorgio Agamben, »Lob der Profanierung«, in: Ders., *Profanierungen*, übers. v. Marianne Schneider, Frankfurt a. M.: Suhrkamp 2005, S. 70–91; die folgenden Zitate stammen aus demselben Essay. Agamben entwickelt den Begriff der Profanierung auch in *Was ist ein Dispositiv?*, übers v. Andreas Hiepko, Zürich und Berlin: Diaphanes 2008 [Orig. 2006]. Er beschäftigt sich jedoch weder mit der materiellen und diskursiven Komplexität eines spezifischen Dispositivs noch mit bestimmten Akten der Profanierung.

Profane Kommunikation

Für Giorgio Agamben besteht die Essenz des Heiligen in der Absonderung. Sie entzieht Dinge, Orte, Handlungen und Menschen der Welt des allgemeinen Gebrauchs und versetzt sie durch Rituale und Mythen in die Sphäre des Göttlichen. »Nicht nur gibt es keine Religion ohne Absonderung, sondern jede Absonderung enthält oder bewahrt in sich einen genuin religiösen Kern.«[14] Diese heilige Absonderung wird auf die Wertform der Ware übertragen, deren Abstraktheit im semiotischen Universum der Finanzmärkte einen Gipfelpunkt erreicht. Doch Agamben fordert nicht die Rückkehr zu einer genuinen Religion. Das dringende Anliegen seines Denkens wird in seinem Begriff der Säkularisierung deutlich:

> Die Säkularisierung ist eine Form von Verdrängung, welche die Kräfte weiterwirken läßt und sich auf deren Verschiebung von einem Ort zum anderen beschränkt. So macht die politische Säkularisierung theologischer Begriffe (die Transzendenz Gottes als souveräne Macht) nichts anderes, als die himmlische Monarchie auf die Erde zu versetzen, läßt deren Macht aber unangetastet.

Der gesamte zeitgenössische Kapitalismus bewirkt eine repressive Säkularisierung, indem er die vollständige Trennung zwischen priesterlichem und säkularem Status in Klassenhierarchien transformiert, in denen die Aura vollständig durch die Ökonomie ersetzt wird. Daher lässt sich die großartige Strategie der Aufklärung, die Entmystifizierung, nicht mehr auf die grundlegenden Machtoperationen unserer Gesellschaften anwenden, die keinen dunklen Kern des Geheimnisvollen mehr enthalten, sondern nur noch obsessive Verfahren zur Auferlegung rationalisierter Mythen und Riten. Anstelle der Säkularisierung schlägt Agamben den Akt der »Profanierung« vor: »Beides sind politische Operationen: aber die erste hat mit der Ausübung der Macht zu tun, die sie gewährleistet, indem sie auf ein heiliges Vorbild zurückführt; die zweite entkräftet die Vorrichtungen der Macht und gibt dem allgemeinen Gebrauch die Räume zurück, welche die Macht konfisziert hatte.«

In Gesellschaften, die von der Mediatisierung zweier destruktiver Rituale – Finanzkrise und Krieg – beherrscht werden, wird der Akt der Profanierung zu einer Notwendigkeit für die Existenz demokratischer Politik. Indem eine frühere Welle von Demonstranten an den Orten globaler Entscheidungsfindung, wie etwa internationalen Gipfeltreffen, zusammenkam, war sie in der Lage, die gesellschaftliche Aufmerksamkeit auf den Ort zu verlagern, an dem sich diese Entscheidungsprozesse konzentrierten und mit den Anordnungen der Macht synchronisierten. Agamben verweist auf eine Art des reinen, funktionsfreien Spiels, das »die Menschheit von der Sphäre des Heiligen befreit und ablenkt, aber ohne sie einfach abzuschaffen«. Dies war die Taktik des »Karnevals gegen Kapital« um die Jahrhundertwende. Doch zu einem Zeitpunkt, an dem die politische Kontrolle Börsenhändlern überlassen wird, die rund um die Uhr, sieben Tage die Woche durch abstrahierende globale Netzwerke operieren, besitzt der Ausbruch des körperlichen Widerspruchs an der Wall Street und in anderen Finanzzentren eine größere Kraft als der Protestkarneval – und dies umso mehr, weil die Besetzungen Tag und Nacht andauern und eher ein anderes Leben verkörpern als ein Störmoment. Der Ausstrahlungseffekt auf die Medien ist enorm. Sobald der Ort der Macht verändert wird, erhält sein Name eine andere Wertigkeit; anstatt an Ohnmacht und zynische Manipulation zu erinnern, wird er zu einer Einladung, die Infragestellung und den Widerstand voranzubringen. Der entscheidende Punkt ist der kulturelle Widerstand gegen die deprimierenden Effekte einer Gesellschaft nach Drehbuch. Um den Charakter des profanen Spiels zu beschreiben, zitiert Agamben den Linguisten Émile Benveniste:

> Die Macht des heiligen Aktes – so schreibt er – liegt in der Verbindung zwischen dem Mythos, der die Geschichte erzählt, und dem Ritus, der sie reproduziert und aufführt. Das Spiel zerbricht diese Einheit: als *ludus* oder handelndes Spiel läßt es den Mythos fallen und bewahrt den Ritus; als *iocus* oder Wortspiel löscht es den Ritus aus und läßt den Mythos überleben. »Wenn sich das Heilige durch die konsubstantielle Einheit von Mythos und Ritus definieren läßt, dann können

wir von einem Spiel sprechen, wenn nur eine Hälfte der heiligen Handlung ausgeführt wird, indem nur der Mythos in Worte oder nur der Ritus in Handlungen übertragen wird.«

Was könnte dies in einem säkularisierten Kontext bedeuten, in dem der Mythos durch die Medien und der Ritus durch die Zweckdienlichkeit mathematischer Modelle und Computerprogramme ersetzt worden sind? Betrachten wir zunächst das erstaunlichste Emblem der jüngsten Besetzungen, nämlich die Schilder. Diese handgeschriebenen Schilder schwanken zwischen einer endlosen Liste von Missständen, einem wütenden »J'accuse!« und einer freundlichen Aufforderung zu satirischer Ungläubigkeit; sie schweben über der Menge wie Überschriften aus dem täglichen Leben und faszinieren die Teilnehmer ebenso wie das Publikum. Diese Schilder sind noch keine Forderungen: Sie sind diskursive und gefühlsbetonte Informationen für die Bewegung selbst und veranschaulichen die kollektive Wahrnehmung gesellschaftlicher Probleme, die von den einflussreichsten Medien zensiert wurden. Ebenso wichtig sind in dieser Hinsicht die – wenn auch nur im Internet veröffentlichten – Briefe der Menschen, die das System im Stich gelassen hat, die Sorgen der 99 Prozent, die es nie bis in eine Statistik geschafft haben.[15] Wortspiele sind bei den Besetzungen allgegenwärtig und ersetzen die schwerfälligen und repressiven Erzeugnisse der Medienkonzerne durch direkte Rede und gemeinschaftliche Erfindung. Der Wille, die Einbahn-Kommunikation zu unterbrechen, ist so stark, dass die Besetzer das »menschliche Mikrofon« sogar dort genutzt haben, wo Verstärker vorhanden und erlaubt waren, um sicherzustellen, dass jedes Wort eines Sprechers am eigenen Leib getestet (und gespürt) werden kann, bevor es als Wahrheit wahrgenommen wird. All dies ereignet sich in Abwesenheit von Fachkenntnissen und jeglichen wie auch immer gearteten »Anforderungen«: Die Verbindung von ideologischem Mythos und instrumentellem Ritus ist unterbrochen. Die Verlagerung und Veröffentlichung von direkter und mediatisierter Rede schafft eine neue Fähigkeit zu kritischer Intelligenz, nicht nur unter den Demonstranten vor Ort, sondern in aller Welt.

Durch die Entstehung einer sozialen Bewegung dient die Analyse der politischen Ökonomie wieder jenen Menschen, die normalerweise auf der Empfängerseite stehen. Das ist etwas Grundlegendes und stellt den bislang größten Gewinn dar. Um jedoch die Abhängigkeit der Intellektuellen und Kulturproduzenten vom Mäzenatentum der Eliten und von Modellen des Humankapitals effektiv zu beenden, muss diese expressive Intelligenz noch stärker in das Berufsleben und die alltägliche Praxis hineingetragen werden. Es gibt eine Respektlosigkeit, die Privilegien und Lügen ausgleicht und durchschneidet; das ist die

15 | http://wearethe99percent.tumblr.com.

Essenz des Profanen. Ein Beispiel: Auf dem Liberty Square hält ein Typ eine Fox-News-Kamera aus Pappe mit einem handgezeichneten, eindimensionalen Mikro, das er beharrlich jedem vor das Gesicht schiebt, der von sich behauptet, wichtig zu sein. Diese Geste löst den Wiederholungszwang der Medien in ein reines Spiel auf: der ethische Ausgangspunkt profaner Kommunikation.

Ein anderer Gebrauch der Rede ist möglich, wenn die Besetzungen den narzisstischen Spiegel zerschlagen, Körper in einer Menge zusammenbringen und ethnische und soziale Grenzen einreißen. Dies ist möglich, weil eine einschneidende Krise des Kapitalismus die unterschiedlichsten Menschen auf die Straße treibt. Die Frage ist, wie man zukünftig mit jenen spricht, die man bis dahin außer Acht gelassen hatte. Unter ihnen könnten sich Wissenschaftler und Techniker befinden, die durch Maschinen Verhaltensweisen prägen, oder Manager, die produktive Kooperationen organisieren. Normalerweise erbringen diese Menschen Dienstleistungen für die Herrschenden. Könnten sie die Verbindung zwischen nützlicher Technologie und mediatisiertem Mythos durchbrechen? Die 68er-Bewegung hatte das Ingenieurwesen, ein zentrales Anliegen des Kommunismus, mehr oder weniger vernachlässigt – mit verheerenden Folgen, denn eine Bewegung ohne *techné* kann niemanden von ihrer Fähigkeit überzeugen, eine Gesellschaft materiell neu zu organisieren. Doch jüngere Aktivisten haben, vor allem durch Netzwerke, einen neuen Zugang zur Technik gefunden. Wenn man den Austausch von Computer-Links von den offiziellen kapitalistischen Ideologien abkoppelt, die diese an das Finanzdispositiv binden, führt dies zur freien Verbreitung eines leistungsstarken Instruments. Ein Beispiel hierfür ist Global Revolution, ein Video-Streaming-Netzwerk. Zu seinen Gründern gehört Vlad Teichberg, der als Zehnjähriger aus Russland in die USA emigrierte. In einem Interview mit *Democracy Now!* spricht er über die Wurzeln von Occupy Wall Street im Arabischen Frühling und in der spanischen Bewegung der Indignados. Diejenigen, die sich über die Kämpfe der Technologen im Inneren des Finanzdispositivs Gedanken machen, können von diesem Mann definitiv etwas lernen:

> Ich war Derivathändler. Ich habe im Wesentlichen für zwei große Banken gearbeitet, mit deren Geld ich auf derivative Produkte gewettet habe. Und mein Job bestand darin zu verstehen, wie diese Produkte funktionieren […]. Für mich […] erwies sich die ganze Globalisierungsphilosophie, die in den frühen und mittleren 1990er Jahren forciert wurde, [die Vorstellung,] dass sie letztlich für mehr Gleichheit in der Welt sorgen würde, aufgrund der Auswirkungen multinationaler Konzerne als falsch. Ich glaube, gegen Ende der 1990er Jahre sind viele Leute zu demselben Schluss gekommen: Die Globalisierung brachte mehr Schaden als Nutzen […]. Und das war auch der Zeitpunkt, als ich anfing, meine Unterstützung für die Ayn-Rand-Sicht der Welt allmählich aufzugeben.[16]

16 | Interview mit Vlad Teichberg, www.democracynow.org/2011/11/18/the_revolution_will_be_live_streamed.

Ein Programmierer wie Teichberg klebt nicht mehr an einer etablierten Verbindung von Diskurs und Praxis. Durch seine Zurückweisung hierarchischer Absonderungen ist er in der Lage, bestimmte Aspekte des Finanzdispositivs für andere Zwecke zu verwenden, um ein planetarisches Netzwerk für den allgemeinen Gebrauch zu schaffen. Das Scheitern der neoliberalen Globalisierung, das für ihn vor zehn Jahren offensichtlich wurde, ist heute für jedermann eine greifbare Tatsache. Plötzlich gibt es ein enormes Potenzial, die Fähigkeiten, die früher dem einen Prozent untergeordnet waren, politisch einzusetzen. Die Widersprüche der »neuen Klasse«, die jahrzehntelang von den Möglichkeiten der finanzialisierten Ökonomie gedämpft wurden, treten erneut in den Vordergrund. Doch die einzige Art, sie lebendig zu halten – und sie davor zu bewahren, vereinnahmt, gelenkt und neutralisiert zu werden –, ist, sie anzuwenden, und zwar nicht nur auf der Straße, sondern auf welchem Gebiet auch immer, das man jeden Tag besetzt. Das Profane ist nur ein Ausgangspunkt. Der Anfang ist nah, wie ein Slogan von Occupy Wall Street besagt.

Die Schließung

Ich begann diesen Text Mitte November 2011 zu schreiben, als in Europa Technokraten die Regierungen übernahmen und in den gesamten USA Robocops die Besetzer gewaltsam vertrieben. Während britische Arbeiter auf einen Generalstreik drängten und chilenische Studenten ihren Aufstand radikalisierten, kamen die Bilder von heroischen Straßenkämpfen auf dem Tahrir-Platz herein. Die »68er-Bewegung« war, wie Wallerstein behauptet hatte, zurück. Es stellte sich heraus, dass das Tränengas für die amerikanische und die ägyptische Polizei aus derselben Fabrik – Combined Systems, Inc. in Jamestown, Pennsylvania – stammte. Auf *Al Jazeera* fand ich einen Text von William Robinson: »Die enormen strukturellen Unterschiede der globalen politischen Ökonomie können nicht länger durch einvernehmliche Mechanismen der gesellschaftlichen Kontrolle ausgeglichen werden. Die herrschenden Klassen haben an Legitimität verloren; wir erleben weltweit einen Zusammenbruch der Hegemonie der herrschenden Klassen.«[17]

Endlich ist offensichtlich geworden, dass sich der Kapitalismus in einer tiefen Krise befindet. Sie wird, wie in den 1930er und 1970er Jahren, nur durch eine Veränderung der grundlegenden Parameter des Systems gelöst werden können. Der entscheidende Punkt ist, sich daran zu beteiligen und eine Handlungsfähigkeit zu entwickeln, die die Dinge zum Besseren wenden kann.

17 | William I. Robinson, »Global Rebellion: The Coming Chaos?«, auf: *Al Jazeera English*, 29. November 2011, www.aljazeera.com/indepth/opinion/2011/11/2011113012155656 7265.html.

Es ist eindrucksvoll zu erfahren, dass eine Expertenkommission von Wirtschaftswissenschaftlern, die für das britische Militär arbeitete, bereits 2007 begriffen hatte, dass »die Mittelschichten [unter dem Druck der Krise] zu einer revolutionären Klasse werden und die Rolle einnehmen könnten, die Marx für das Proletariat voraussah«. Sie schrieben:

> Die Globalisierung der Arbeitsmärkte und das Sinken von nationalen Sozialleistungen und Beschäftigung könnte die Bindung der Bevölkerung an bestimmte Staaten verringern. Die zunehmende Kluft zwischen ihr und einer kleinen Gruppe von höchst sichtbaren superreichen Einzelpersonen könnte die Enttäuschung über die Leistungsgesellschaft schüren, während die wachsenden urbanen Unterschichten wahrscheinlich eine steigende Bedrohung der gesellschaftlichen Ordnung und Stabilität darstellen, sobald die Last übernommener Schulden und die Versäumnisse bei der Altersvorsorge zu greifen beginnen. Mit dieser doppelten Herausforderung konfrontiert, könnten sich die Mittelschichten in aller Welt zusammenschließen und ihren Zugang zu Wissen, Ressourcen und Fähigkeiten nutzen, um transnationale Prozesse im Interesse ihrer eigenen Schicht umzugestalten.[18]

Jetzt beginnen solche Zukunftsaussichten, Wirklichkeit zu werden – und werden umgehend vom Kapital-Staat unterdrückt. Die Frage ist, was als Nächstes passiert. Können Intellektuelle und Kulturproduzenten des Nordens, die parallel zu ihren Gleichgesinnten im Süden agieren, zu einer Widerstandsbewegung gegen Ungleichheit und Unterdrückung von der Größenordnung der Weltrevolution des Jahres 1968 beitragen? Können wir die von der Wirtschaftskrise ausgelöste Solidarität nutzen, um die gegenwärtige Hegemonie zu transformieren? Können wir auf neuartige Weise intervenieren, um nicht eine gewaltsame Reaktion zu provozieren, sondern vielmehr eine positive strukturelle Veränderung jener repressiven Entwicklung zu bewirken, die derzeit als »Nekropolitik« bezeichnet wird?[19]

Aufstände in Nordamerika und Europa werden sich, vor allem aufgrund der dauerhaften geopolitischen Ungleichheit, immer anders artikulieren als solche in Ländern wie Ägypten oder Tunesien. Das geheime Bindeglied zwischen unseren sich überkreuzenden Geschichten ist jedoch, dass wir letztlich dieselben Gegner haben. Hinter der Wunschmaschine der Finanzmärkte lauert die Autorität der Generäle. Dies war während des zurückliegenden Jahrzehnts, als auf die Dotcom-Pleite eine globale Sicherheitspanik und zwei brutale Kriege folgten, offensichtlich; doch in einer Zeit engster Komplizenschaft zwischen den Mittelschichten und unseren habgierigen Eliten verlief das alltägliche Leben weiterhin ungestört. Es geht darum, sich von den Imperativen des einen Prozents loszureißen, das die öffentlichen Institutionen umgestaltet und die kulturelle und intellektuelle Sphäre sehr stark durchdrungen hat. Zu diesem Zweck muss man ein anderes Spiel spielen, das nicht länger eine Wette ist. Ohne den

18 | »The DCDC Global Strategic Trends Programme, 2007–2036«, www.frequencyclear.tv/strat_trends.pdf.

19 | Achille Mbembe, »Necropolitics«, in: *Public Culture*, 15, Nr. 1, 2003, www.jhfc.duke.edu/icuss/pdfs/Mbembe.pdf.

greifbaren Beweis einer veränderten Loyalität – der im Wesentlichen durch Projekte erbracht wird, die außerhalb der professionellen Ökonomie entstehen – kann man das Vertrauen anderer nicht gewinnen. Ohne die Fähigkeit, in etablierte Bereiche und Arbeitsplätze hineinzuwirken – die man im Wesentlichen erreicht, indem man philosophische Grundsätze mutig gegen die herrschenden Regeln verteidigt –, ist es unmöglich, die Fähigkeit zum gesellschaftlichen Wandel zu erlangen.

Die wachsenden Managerklassen des Südens sind bereits mit ähnlichen Dilemmas konfrontiert. Eine wichtige Einsicht findet sich in den Aufzeichnungen von Mark LeVine, einem jungen Professor an der University of California, der Zeuge der Ereignisse in Ägypten wurde. In einem Bericht über einen mitternächtlichen Besuch auf dem Tahrir-Platz spricht er über den Wunsch der informellen »Anführer« der Bewegung, dort einen Raum für die Dichtung, Musik, Filme und anderen Formen von Kultur zu gründen, die den Aufstand von Beginn an mitgetragen haben:

> Mit anderen Worten, die Anführer vom Tahrir-Platz möchten die unglaubliche Kreativität der Revolution, von Musikaufführungen und Filmen bis zu Kunstwerken, Gedichten und Erzählungen, institutionalisieren. Diese Aktivitäten haben die Protestierenden in den dunkelsten Tagen der Gewalt unterstützt und dazu beigetragen, dass der Platz der Befreiung während der Besetzungen seit Januar jedes Mal Hunderttausende »normaler Ägypter« anzog. Dies würde ein dauerhaftes Gegengewicht zu den staatlichen Medien und anderen Mechanismen schaffen, die der Regierung und der Elite zur Verfügung stehen, um die Ägypter womöglich davon zu überzeugen, dass die Demonstranten auf dem Tahrir-Platz nichts als »Gangster« sind, denen ihre Interessen nicht am Herzen liegen.[20]

In den korrupten und verfallenden Ländern des Nordens müssen Künstler und Intellektuelle diesen Wunsch nach einer Kultur außerhalb des finanzialisierten Staates erst noch wiederentdecken – eine profane Kultur, die stark, anspruchsvoll und tiefgründig, aber offen für den allgemeinen Gebrauch ist. Nur so können wir die Affekte des Widerstands stärken und die Fähigkeit entwickeln, Alternativen zu schaffen. Und es gibt keine Zeit für Ambivalenzen. Eine Strukturkrise lässt sich nur durch tiefgreifende Veränderungen bewältigen, was immer auch geschehen mag. Es ist unausweichlich, dass soziale Bewegungen eingreifen, aber oft mit ungewollten Folgen, wie sich in den Nixon-Jahren herausstellte. Die heutige Herausforderung in Gesellschaften, in denen die alternden und ängstlichen Reichen dominieren, besteht darin, trotzig auf einen ökonomischen und ökologischen Wandel zu drängen und dabei die Polizeigewalt fernzuhalten. Wahrscheinlich wird dies irgendwann in den kommenden Jahren ein entschiedenes Handeln erfordern, wie in jenen Tagen, als die Menschen im ehemaligen Osten auf die Straße gingen und sie nicht mehr

20 | Mark LeVine, »Tahrir's Late Night Conversations«, auf: *Al Jazeera English*, 5. Dezember 2011, www.aljazeera.com/indepth/opinion/2011/12/201112511219971906.html.

Alle Internetseiten abgerufen am 15. Dezember 2011.

verließen. Aber das Hoffen allein wird nicht helfen – denn wenn das Finanzchaos wirklich ausbricht, haben die Generäle einen Plan.

Klassenstrategien entstehen aus der Häufung kleiner Entscheidungen. Fragen Sie sich selbst und fragen Sie die Menschen in Ihrer Umgebung, was *wir* tun müssen, um das Casino zu schließen.

Dieser Text entstand für ein selbstorganisiertes Seminar mit dem Titel »Three Crises: 30s – 70s – Today«. Das Archiv des gesamten Seminars ist abrufbar unter http://messhall.org.

Brian Holmes ist Kulturkritiker und unabhängiger Forscher; er lebt in Chicago.

100 Notes – 100 Thoughts / 100 Notizen – 100 Gedanken

Nº064: Brian Holmes
Profanity and the Financial Markets: A User's Guide to Closing the Casino / Das Profane und die Finanzmärkte. Eine Gebrauchsanleitung zur Schließung des Casinos

dOCUMENTA (13), 9/6/2012 – 16/9/2012
Artistic Director / Künstlerische Leiterin: Carolyn Christov-Bakargiev
Member of Core Agent Group, Head of Department /
Mitglied der Agenten-Kerngruppe, Leiterin der Abteilung: Chus Martínez
Head of Publications / Leiterin der Publikationsabteilung: Bettina Funcke

Managing Editor / Redaktion und Lektorat: Katrin Sauerländer
Editorial Assistant / Redaktionsassistentin: Cordelia Marten
Copyediting / Lektorat: Melissa Larner, Alexander Müller
Proofreading / Korrektorat: Stefanie Drobnik, Sam Frank
Translation / Übersetzung: Barbara Hess
Image Editing / Bildredaktion: Frauke Schnoor
Graphic Design and Typesetting / Grafische Gestaltung und Satz: Leftloft
Junior Graphic Designer: Daniela Weirich
Typeface / Schrift: Glypha, Plantin
Production / Verlagsherstellung: Maren Katrin Poppe
Reproductions / Reproduktionen: weyhing digital, Ostfildern
Paper / Papier: Pop'Set, 240 g/m², Munken Print Cream 15, 90 g/m²
Manufacturing / Gesamtherstellung: Dr. Cantz'sche Druckerei, Ostfildern

Illustrations / Abbildungen: p. / S. 1: Students on deck of Chalet III (Farrally Hall) / Studenten auf der Terrasse des Chalet III (Farrally Hall), The Banff Centre, 1956 (detail / Detail), courtesy Paul D. Fleck Library & Archives at The Banff Centre;
p. / S. 2: ddp images/AP/Andrew Burton

documenta und Museum Fridericianum Veranstaltungs-GmbH
Friedrichsplatz 18, 34117 Kassel
Germany / Deutschland
Tel. +49 561 70727-0
Fax +49 561 70727-39
www.documenta.de
Chief Executive Officer / Geschäftsführer: Bernd Leifeld

Published by / Erschienen im
Hatje Cantz Verlag
Zeppelinstrasse 32, 73760 Ostfildern
Germany / Deutschland
Tel. +49 711 4405-200
Fax +49 711 4405-220
www.hatjecantz.com

ISBN 978-3-7757-2913-0 (Print)
ISBN 978-3-7757-3093-8 (E-Book)

Printed in Germany

Gefördert durch die

KULTURSTIFTUNG DES BUNDES

funded by the German Federal Cultural Foundation